MONTHLY

BOOKKEEPING BOOK

SPEEDY
PUBLISHING

Speedy Publishing LLC
40 E. Main St. #1156
Newark, DE 19711

www.SpeedyPublishing.Com

MONTHLY EXPENDITURE

MERCHANDISE & MATERIALS				OTHER EXPENSES			
DATE	**CHECK #**	**PAID TO**	**AMOUNT**	**DATE**	**CHECK #**	**PAID TO**	**AMOUNT**
		TOTAL				**TOTAL**	

MONTHLY EXPENDITURE

MERCHANDISE & MATERIALS				OTHER EXPENSES			
DATE	**CHECK #**	**PAID TO**	**AMOUNT**	**DATE**	**CHECK #**	**PAID TO**	**AMOUNT**
TOTAL FROM PREVIOUS PAGE				TOTAL FROM PREVIOUS PAGE			
		TOTAL				**TOTAL**	

MONTHLY EXPENDITURE

MERCHANDISE & MATERIALS			
DATE	**CHECK #**	**PAID TO**	**AMOUNT**
TOTAL FROM PREVIOUS PAGE			
		TOTAL	

OTHER EXPENSES			
DATE	**CHECK #**	**PAID TO**	**AMOUNT**
TOTAL FROM PREVIOUS PAGE			
		TOTAL	

MONTHLY EXPENDITURE

MERCHANDISE & MATERIALS				OTHER EXPENSES			
DATE	**CHECK #**	**PAID TO**	**AMOUNT**	**DATE**	**CHECK #**	**PAID TO**	**AMOUNT**
TOTAL FROM PREVIOUS PAGE				TOTAL FROM PREVIOUS PAGE			
		TOTAL				**TOTAL**	

MONTHLY EXPENDITURE

MERCHANDISE & MATERIALS

DATE	CHECK #	PAID TO	AMOUNT
TOTAL FROM PREVIOUS PAGE			
		TOTAL	

OTHER EXPENSES

DATE	CHECK #	PAID TO	AMOUNT
TOTAL FROM PREVIOUS PAGE			
		TOTAL	

MONTHLY EXPENDITURE

MERCHANDISE & MATERIALS			
DATE	**CHECK #**	**PAID TO**	**AMOUNT**
TOTAL FROM PREVIOUS PAGE			
		TOTAL	

OTHER EXPENSES			
DATE	**CHECK #**	**PAID TO**	**AMOUNT**
TOTAL FROM PREVIOUS PAGE			
		TOTAL	

MONTHLY EXPENDITURE

MERCHANDISE & MATERIALS				OTHER EXPENSES			
DATE	**CHECK #**	**PAID TO**	**AMOUNT**	**DATE**	**CHECK #**	**PAID TO**	**AMOUNT**
TOTAL FROM PREVIOUS PAGE				TOTAL FROM PREVIOUS PAGE			
		TOTAL				**TOTAL**	

MONTHLY EXPENDITURE

MERCHANDISE & MATERIALS

DATE	CHECK #	PAID TO	AMOUNT
TOTAL FROM PREVIOUS PAGE			
		TOTAL	

OTHER EXPENSES

DATE	CHECK #	PAID TO	AMOUNT
TOTAL FROM PREVIOUS PAGE			
		TOTAL	

MONTHLY EXPENDITURE

MERCHANDISE & MATERIALS				OTHER EXPENSES			
DATE	**CHECK #**	**PAID TO**	**AMOUNT**	**DATE**	**CHECK #**	**PAID TO**	**AMOUNT**
TOTAL FROM PREVIOUS PAGE				TOTAL FROM PREVIOUS PAGE			
		TOTAL				**TOTAL**	

MONTHLY EXPENDITURE

MERCHANDISE & MATERIALS				OTHER EXPENSES			
DATE	**CHECK #**	**PAID TO**	**AMOUNT**	**DATE**	**CHECK #**	**PAID TO**	**AMOUNT**
TOTAL FROM PREVIOUS PAGE				TOTAL FROM PREVIOUS PAGE			
		TOTAL				**TOTAL**	

MONTHLY EXPENDITURE

MERCHANDISE & MATERIALS

DATE	CHECK #	PAID TO	AMOUNT
TOTAL FROM PREVIOUS PAGE			
		TOTAL	

OTHER EXPENSES

DATE	CHECK #	PAID TO	AMOUNT
TOTAL FROM PREVIOUS PAGE			
		TOTAL	

MONTHLY EXPENDITURE

MERCHANDISE & MATERIALS

DATE	CHECK #	PAID TO	AMOUNT
TOTAL FROM PREVIOUS PAGE			
		TOTAL	

OTHER EXPENSES

DATE	CHECK #	PAID TO	AMOUNT
TOTAL FROM PREVIOUS PAGE			
		TOTAL	

MONTHLY EXPENDITURE

MERCHANDISE & MATERIALS				OTHER EXPENSES			
DATE	**CHECK #**	**PAID TO**	**AMOUNT**	**DATE**	**CHECK #**	**PAID TO**	**AMOUNT**
TOTAL FROM PREVIOUS PAGE				TOTAL FROM PREVIOUS PAGE			
		TOTAL				**TOTAL**	

MONTHLY EXPENDITURE

MERCHANDISE & MATERIALS

DATE	CHECK #	PAID TO	AMOUNT
TOTAL FROM PREVIOUS PAGE			
		TOTAL	

OTHER EXPENSES

DATE	CHECK #	PAID TO	AMOUNT
TOTAL FROM PREVIOUS PAGE			
		TOTAL	

MONTHLY EXPENDITURE

MERCHANDISE & MATERIALS				OTHER EXPENSES			
DATE	**CHECK #**	**PAID TO**	**AMOUNT**	**DATE**	**CHECK #**	**PAID TO**	**AMOUNT**
TOTAL FROM PREVIOUS PAGE				TOTAL FROM PREVIOUS PAGE			
		TOTAL				**TOTAL**	

MONTHLY EXPENDITURE

MERCHANDISE & MATERIALS				OTHER EXPENSES			
DATE	**CHECK #**	**PAID TO**	**AMOUNT**	**DATE**	**CHECK #**	**PAID TO**	**AMOUNT**
TOTAL FROM PREVIOUS PAGE				TOTAL FROM PREVIOUS PAGE			
		TOTAL				**TOTAL**	

MONTHLY EXPENDITURE

MERCHANDISE & MATERIALS				OTHER EXPENSES			
DATE	**CHECK #**	**PAID TO**	**AMOUNT**	**DATE**	**CHECK #**	**PAID TO**	**AMOUNT**
TOTAL FROM PREVIOUS PAGE				TOTAL FROM PREVIOUS PAGE			
		TOTAL				**TOTAL**	

MONTHLY EXPENDITURE

MERCHANDISE & MATERIALS

DATE	CHECK #	PAID TO	AMOUNT
TOTAL FROM PREVIOUS PAGE			
		TOTAL	

OTHER EXPENSES

DATE	CHECK #	PAID TO	AMOUNT
TOTAL FROM PREVIOUS PAGE			
		TOTAL	

MONTHLY EXPENDITURE

MERCHANDISE & MATERIALS				OTHER EXPENSES			
DATE	**CHECK #**	**PAID TO**	**AMOUNT**	**DATE**	**CHECK #**	**PAID TO**	**AMOUNT**
TOTAL FROM PREVIOUS PAGE				TOTAL FROM PREVIOUS PAGE			
		TOTAL				**TOTAL**	

MONTHLY EXPENDITURE

MERCHANDISE & MATERIALS

DATE	CHECK #	PAID TO	AMOUNT
TOTAL FROM PREVIOUS PAGE			
		TOTAL	

OTHER EXPENSES

DATE	CHECK #	PAID TO	AMOUNT
TOTAL FROM PREVIOUS PAGE			
		TOTAL	

MONTHLY EXPENDITURE

MERCHANDISE & MATERIALS				OTHER EXPENSES			
DATE	**CHECK #**	**PAID TO**	**AMOUNT**	**DATE**	**CHECK #**	**PAID TO**	**AMOUNT**
TOTAL FROM PREVIOUS PAGE				TOTAL FROM PREVIOUS PAGE			
		TOTAL				**TOTAL**	

MONTHLY EXPENDITURE

MERCHANDISE & MATERIALS				OTHER EXPENSES			
DATE	**CHECK #**	**PAID TO**	**AMOUNT**	**DATE**	**CHECK #**	**PAID TO**	**AMOUNT**
TOTAL FROM PREVIOUS PAGE				TOTAL FROM PREVIOUS PAGE			
		TOTAL				**TOTAL**	

MONTHLY EXPENDITURE

MERCHANDISE & MATERIALS				OTHER EXPENSES			
DATE	**CHECK #**	**PAID TO**	**AMOUNT**	**DATE**	**CHECK #**	**PAID TO**	**AMOUNT**
TOTAL FROM PREVIOUS PAGE				TOTAL FROM PREVIOUS PAGE			
		TOTAL				**TOTAL**	

MONTHLY EXPENDITURE

MERCHANDISE & MATERIALS				OTHER EXPENSES			
DATE	**CHECK #**	**PAID TO**	**AMOUNT**	**DATE**	**CHECK #**	**PAID TO**	**AMOUNT**
TOTAL FROM PREVIOUS PAGE				TOTAL FROM PREVIOUS PAGE			
		TOTAL				**TOTAL**	

MONTHLY EXPENDITURE

MERCHANDISE & MATERIALS				OTHER EXPENSES			
DATE	**CHECK #**	**PAID TO**	**AMOUNT**	**DATE**	**CHECK #**	**PAID TO**	**AMOUNT**
TOTAL FROM PREVIOUS PAGE				TOTAL FROM PREVIOUS PAGE			
		TOTAL				**TOTAL**	

MONTHLY EXPENDITURE

MERCHANDISE & MATERIALS				OTHER EXPENSES			
DATE	**CHECK #**	**PAID TO**	**AMOUNT**	**DATE**	**CHECK #**	**PAID TO**	**AMOUNT**
TOTAL FROM PREVIOUS PAGE				TOTAL FROM PREVIOUS PAGE			
		TOTAL				**TOTAL**	

MONTHLY EXPENDITURE

MERCHANDISE & MATERIALS				OTHER EXPENSES			
DATE	**CHECK #**	**PAID TO**	**AMOUNT**	**DATE**	**CHECK #**	**PAID TO**	**AMOUNT**
TOTAL FROM PREVIOUS PAGE				TOTAL FROM PREVIOUS PAGE			
		TOTAL				**TOTAL**	

MONTHLY EXPENDITURE

MERCHANDISE & MATERIALS				OTHER EXPENSES			
DATE	**CHECK #**	**PAID TO**	**AMOUNT**	**DATE**	**CHECK #**	**PAID TO**	**AMOUNT**
TOTAL FROM PREVIOUS PAGE				TOTAL FROM PREVIOUS PAGE			
		TOTAL				**TOTAL**	

MONTHLY EXPENDITURE

MERCHANDISE & MATERIALS

DATE	CHECK #	PAID TO	AMOUNT
TOTAL FROM PREVIOUS PAGE			
		TOTAL	

OTHER EXPENSES

DATE	CHECK #	PAID TO	AMOUNT
TOTAL FROM PREVIOUS PAGE			
		TOTAL	

MONTHLY EXPENDITURE

MERCHANDISE & MATERIALS				OTHER EXPENSES			
DATE	**CHECK #**	**PAID TO**	**AMOUNT**	**DATE**	**CHECK #**	**PAID TO**	**AMOUNT**
TOTAL FROM PREVIOUS PAGE				TOTAL FROM PREVIOUS PAGE			
		TOTAL				**TOTAL**	

MONTHLY EXPENDITURE

MERCHANDISE & MATERIALS				OTHER EXPENSES			
DATE	**CHECK #**	**PAID TO**	**AMOUNT**	**DATE**	**CHECK #**	**PAID TO**	**AMOUNT**
TOTAL FROM PREVIOUS PAGE				TOTAL FROM PREVIOUS PAGE			
		TOTAL				**TOTAL**	

MONTHLY EXPENDITURE

MERCHANDISE & MATERIALS				OTHER EXPENSES			
DATE	**CHECK #**	**PAID TO**	**AMOUNT**	**DATE**	**CHECK #**	**PAID TO**	**AMOUNT**
TOTAL FROM PREVIOUS PAGE				TOTAL FROM PREVIOUS PAGE			
		TOTAL				**TOTAL**	

MONTHLY EXPENDITURE

MERCHANDISE & MATERIALS				OTHER EXPENSES			
DATE	**CHECK #**	**PAID TO**	**AMOUNT**	**DATE**	**CHECK #**	**PAID TO**	**AMOUNT**
TOTAL FROM PREVIOUS PAGE				TOTAL FROM PREVIOUS PAGE			
		TOTAL				**TOTAL**	

MONTHLY EXPENDITURE

MERCHANDISE & MATERIALS

DATE	CHECK #	PAID TO	AMOUNT
TOTAL FROM PREVIOUS PAGE			
		TOTAL	

OTHER EXPENSES

DATE	CHECK #	PAID TO	AMOUNT
TOTAL FROM PREVIOUS PAGE			
		TOTAL	

MONTHLY EXPENDITURE

MERCHANDISE & MATERIALS			
DATE	**CHECK #**	**PAID TO**	**AMOUNT**
TOTAL FROM PREVIOUS PAGE			
		TOTAL	

OTHER EXPENSES			
DATE	**CHECK #**	**PAID TO**	**AMOUNT**
TOTAL FROM PREVIOUS PAGE			
		TOTAL	

MONTHLY EXPENDITURE

MERCHANDISE & MATERIALS			
DATE	**CHECK #**	**PAID TO**	**AMOUNT**
TOTAL FROM PREVIOUS PAGE			
		TOTAL	

OTHER EXPENSES			
DATE	**CHECK #**	**PAID TO**	**AMOUNT**
TOTAL FROM PREVIOUS PAGE			
		TOTAL	

MONTHLY EXPENDITURE

MERCHANDISE & MATERIALS				OTHER EXPENSES			
DATE	**CHECK #**	**PAID TO**	**AMOUNT**	**DATE**	**CHECK #**	**PAID TO**	**AMOUNT**
TOTAL FROM PREVIOUS PAGE				TOTAL FROM PREVIOUS PAGE			
		TOTAL				**TOTAL**	

MONTHLY EXPENDITURE

MERCHANDISE & MATERIALS

DATE	CHECK #	PAID TO	AMOUNT
TOTAL FROM PREVIOUS PAGE			
		TOTAL	

OTHER EXPENSES

DATE	CHECK #	PAID TO	AMOUNT
TOTAL FROM PREVIOUS PAGE			
		TOTAL	

MONTHLY EXPENDITURE

MERCHANDISE & MATERIALS

DATE	CHECK #	PAID TO	AMOUNT
TOTAL FROM PREVIOUS PAGE			
		TOTAL	

OTHER EXPENSES

DATE	CHECK #	PAID TO	AMOUNT
TOTAL FROM PREVIOUS PAGE			
		TOTAL	

MONTHLY EXPENDITURE

MERCHANDISE & MATERIALS

DATE	CHECK #	PAID TO	AMOUNT
TOTAL FROM PREVIOUS PAGE			
		TOTAL	

OTHER EXPENSES

DATE	CHECK #	PAID TO	AMOUNT
TOTAL FROM PREVIOUS PAGE			
		TOTAL	

MONTHLY EXPENDITURE

MERCHANDISE & MATERIALS				OTHER EXPENSES			
DATE	CHECK #	PAID TO	AMOUNT	DATE	CHECK #	PAID TO	AMOUNT
TOTAL FROM PREVIOUS PAGE				TOTAL FROM PREVIOUS PAGE			
		TOTAL				TOTAL	

MONTHLY EXPENDITURE

MERCHANDISE & MATERIALS				OTHER EXPENSES			
DATE	**CHECK #**	**PAID TO**	**AMOUNT**	**DATE**	**CHECK #**	**PAID TO**	**AMOUNT**
TOTAL FROM PREVIOUS PAGE				TOTAL FROM PREVIOUS PAGE			
		TOTAL				**TOTAL**	

MONTHLY EXPENDITURE

MERCHANDISE & MATERIALS

DATE	CHECK #	PAID TO	AMOUNT
TOTAL FROM PREVIOUS PAGE			
		TOTAL	

OTHER EXPENSES

DATE	CHECK #	PAID TO	AMOUNT
TOTAL FROM PREVIOUS PAGE			
		TOTAL	

MONTHLY EXPENDITURE

MERCHANDISE & MATERIALS

DATE	CHECK #	PAID TO	AMOUNT
TOTAL FROM PREVIOUS PAGE			
		TOTAL	

OTHER EXPENSES

DATE	CHECK #	PAID TO	AMOUNT
TOTAL FROM PREVIOUS PAGE			
		TOTAL	

MONTHLY EXPENDITURE

MERCHANDISE & MATERIALS

DATE	CHECK #	PAID TO	AMOUNT
TOTAL FROM PREVIOUS PAGE			
		TOTAL	

OTHER EXPENSES

DATE	CHECK #	PAID TO	AMOUNT
TOTAL FROM PREVIOUS PAGE			
		TOTAL	

MONTHLY EXPENDITURE

MERCHANDISE & MATERIALS				OTHER EXPENSES			
DATE	**CHECK #**	**PAID TO**	**AMOUNT**	**DATE**	**CHECK #**	**PAID TO**	**AMOUNT**
TOTAL FROM PREVIOUS PAGE				TOTAL FROM PREVIOUS PAGE			
		TOTAL				**TOTAL**	

MONTHLY EXPENDITURE

MERCHANDISE & MATERIALS

DATE	CHECK #	PAID TO	AMOUNT
TOTAL FROM PREVIOUS PAGE			
		TOTAL	

OTHER EXPENSES

DATE	CHECK #	PAID TO	AMOUNT
TOTAL FROM PREVIOUS PAGE			
		TOTAL	

MONTHLY EXPENDITURE

MERCHANDISE & MATERIALS

DATE	CHECK #	PAID TO	AMOUNT
TOTAL FROM PREVIOUS PAGE			
		TOTAL	

OTHER EXPENSES

DATE	CHECK #	PAID TO	AMOUNT
TOTAL FROM PREVIOUS PAGE			
		TOTAL	

MONTHLY EXPENDITURE

MERCHANDISE & MATERIALS

DATE	CHECK #	PAID TO	AMOUNT
TOTAL FROM PREVIOUS PAGE			
		TOTAL	

OTHER EXPENSES

DATE	CHECK #	PAID TO	AMOUNT
TOTAL FROM PREVIOUS PAGE			
		TOTAL	

MONTHLY EXPENDITURE

MERCHANDISE & MATERIALS

DATE	CHECK #	PAID TO	AMOUNT
TOTAL FROM PREVIOUS PAGE			
		TOTAL	

OTHER EXPENSES

DATE	CHECK #	PAID TO	AMOUNT
TOTAL FROM PREVIOUS PAGE			
		TOTAL	

MONTHLY EXPENDITURE

MERCHANDISE & MATERIALS				OTHER EXPENSES			
DATE	**CHECK #**	**PAID TO**	**AMOUNT**	**DATE**	**CHECK #**	**PAID TO**	**AMOUNT**
TOTAL FROM PREVIOUS PAGE				TOTAL FROM PREVIOUS PAGE			
		TOTAL				**TOTAL**	

www.ingramcontent.com/pod-product-compliance
Lightning Source LLC
LaVergne TN
LVHW082354200926
848481LV00012B/3564